C000293939

THE ARCTIC

by the same author

poetry
NIL NIL
GOD'S GIFT TO WOMEN
THE EYES
LANDING LIGHT
ORPHEUS
RAIN
SELECTED POEMS
40 SONNETS
ZONAL

aphorism
THE BOOK OF SHADOWS
THE BLIND EYE
THE FALL AT HOME

criticism and literary theory
READING SHAKESPEARE'S SONNETS
SMITH: A READER'S GUIDE TO THE POETRY OF MICHAEL DONAGHY
THE POEM: LYRIC, SIGN, METRE

as editor (selected)
ROBERT BURNS: SELECTED POEMS
101 SONNETS
THE ZOO OF THE NEW (*with* Nick Laird)
NEW BRITISH POETRY (*with* Charles Simic)
TRAIN SONGS (*with* Sean O'Brien)
DON'T ASK ME WHAT I MEAN (*with* Clare Brown)
THE GOLDEN TREASURY OF SCOTTISH VERSE
(*with* Kathleen Jamie, Peter Mackay)

DON PATERSON

The Arctic

faber

First published in 2022
by Faber & Faber Ltd
Bloomsbury House
74–77 Great Russell Street
London WC1B 3DA

Typeset by Hamish Ironside
Printed in the UK by TJ Books Ltd, Padstow, Cornwall

All rights reserved
© Don Paterson, 2022

The right of Don Paterson to be identified as author
of this work has been asserted in accordance with Section 77
of the Copyright, Designs and Patents Act 1988

A CIP record for this book is available from the British Library

ISBN 978-0-571-33818-4

FSC
www.fsc.org
MIX
Paper from
responsible sources
FSC® C013056

2 4 6 8 10 9 7 5 3

for my brother and sister

Acknowledgements

The author is grateful to the editors and curators of the various journals, radio programmes and exhibitions in which earlier versions of some of these poems originally appeared. 'Spring Letter' was first published in *Prospect*, and a version of 'Ten Maxims' in *A New Divan*. 'The Alexandrian Library, Part IV: Citizen Science' was written as part of the AHRC-funded Constructing Scientific Communities project; some of the research projects described here explicitly refer to those hosted on the Zooniverse citizen science web portal.

Contents

THE ARCTIC

El hombre que no se aflige apenas existe.

– Antonio Porchia

Repertoire

The last few times he dragged his box along
to the folk club upstairs at the Brig O' Tay
until the night the stairs turned him away
he told me he could get right through a song
by forgetting his hands, and fixing on the space
above the sea-line, so its empty plane
could clear the garbled switchboard in his brain
of any tune not soldered into place.
In the end, he'd only two left in the book
whose names I might be tempted to curate
for their piquancy, had he not put me straight:
'It's not a violin.' From which I took
you play the crowd, or play whatever's true.
('Truck Drivin' Man' and 'Good Old Mountain Dew'.)

Snaba

I hadn't heard the word in forty years
until then, at the ragged hem of sleep,
just once, in his bedside voice: that word
only he would call me by, and only
when I was sick, or cried out from a dream.
Why would he console me with it now?
I'd put three whole years on that rainy month
his death seemed almost lost in all the trouble.
Why so out of time? Although the dead
don't know to keep the order of our days.

But perhaps one doesn't ever really mourn
those obliged to leave us by degrees;
our last tears are relief, if there are any.
The blessing of a death to take him clean
was denied that man of purely good intention
who left us through a puncture in his side,
a slow leak hissing all that made him him –
I will say *soul* – back to the receiving dark
from which it first had calved, then found its host.
It was a stronger vessel than he needed.

His sickness was a stair into a cellar
where not one thing had edge enough to name;
but the steps were shallow and he took them slow,
so mostly I was dead to it, and dry-eyed
bar perhaps the last time he restrung
his good guitar, and everything was backwards
and upside down and him weeping in anger.
O Dad. But otherwise. Eventually
he slept, if we discount that last astonishment
I'd only seen before on the just-born.

Snaba. From before I could remember
a name so often mine I barely knew it,
although all names are strange, so long unused.
Back then, all I heard was the love in it,
the way his father too had called him by
the same Mearns pet-word, maybe from the Norse,
meaning child, or beloved one. The last time
I was sixteen, and shivering and raving
in the last bed in the ward, when I thought
they were all trying to kill me. *Snaba*, he'd said.

Of course. Now that it's all I have of him
it's so obvious, I could laugh. *Snaa' ba'*.
'Snowball.' That was all that he was calling me
in his own childhood Scots. And now the boy
with the white hair and the white beard holds
his knees and makes himself very small and round
because now he is very cold and he has no father.

Air Guitar

This year we've had to arm his good guitar
with super-lights, harp-wire and gossamer –
but now there's nothing at his fingertips

God only knows the chords that lie below
the vague reflexive clutchings that he makes
when I put the neck into his severed hands.

Test

So for the record: when we die
our hearts don't slow like steps or clocks
but whirr like small wings in a box
now lit up by a crack of sky.

Money

Even now, I tune
each new string to its neighbour
tensed for that dull snap –
his were always so heavy
and he was too broke for spares

On Sounding Good

i.m. Russell L. Paterson

Sir, know this: that you were utter shite
in the Kirkintilloch Social Club that night
when at the bidding of your next of kin
you rushed the stage and counted yourself in,
resolved to give it laldy, your best shot,
all you had and more that you did not,
on a number you'd pinpointed in advance
with a misplaced yet granitic confidence
and a mondegreen of two words which belonged
to the chorus of a wholly different song;
and yet my father, on your one-two-three
took one breath to exhume your opening key
then shadowed you as with Apollo's harp
through your ascent from E flat to K sharp.

But you barely heard the man with the guitar
who guided you towards the final bar
and off into the safety of the wing
like the Dalai Lama gently shepherding
a drunken wasp towards an open window,
nor, as you reached your bestial crescendo
did you see just how his providence had lent
the guise of logic to each chance event,
a velvet tray of right made for the wrong
that was the alien spanners of your song.

He did all this because he had an ear
like the sea that raised him, open, true and clear;
so on that night, as every night, he chose
to make you sound good, or good at least to those
who loved you; and since he had love to spare,
your knowing this was neither here nor there.

I am not me

after Juan Ramón Jiménez

I am not me. I am the one
who walks unseen beside me.
The one I sense, from time to time,
but often forget; the one
who is silent and still while I'm speaking;
who forgives me when I'm spiteful;
who is where I am not;
who will stay standing when I finally lie down.

The Customs House

after Montale

You don't remember the customs house
on the clifftop, overhanging the reef?
Long abandoned, it's been waiting for you
since that evening the swarm of your worries
first poured inside, and settled there so restlessly.

Sou'westers have thrashed the old walls for years
while your laughter turned hollow.
The compass-needle spins in an unseen storm,
and the dice won't add up . . . You don't
remember, do you? Some other time
is tugging on the memory like a thread.

Still, I grip one end. But the customs house
is dwindling, its smoke-black weathervane
spinning, spinning mercilessly –
I grip the thread, but you remain alone,
not breathing, here in the darkness.

O how the horizon shrinks back from itself
out where the oil tankers flare, less and less . . .
Is this the way through? (The breakers seethe
against the plunging cliffs forever . . .)
You don't remember it, do you? The house of this,
    my evening.
And I do not know who is leaving, or who must stay.

The Sicilian Advantage

For me? You shouldn't have. No, I mean it.
I hate surprises. But this is. Apropos.
Not sure how you knew but anyways,
thank you. Yes I'm here most nights these days
with the house red and the vitello Milanese.
Don't say *creature of habit*. Makes it sound lazy,
it's an economy. No more for me no –
it's fine, stop fussing. I'll have Ugo clean it.
Yeah, same table, parked here like a rook.
Au cont, it's more like my idea of freedom –
you remember my bed that one time, in the nook,
the pillows in the corner. *God* no. Never.
But tell me about your weekend or whatever.
Just keep your hands up here where I can see them.

I am Sleepy

From my troubles, now, and for some light relief
confuse the Seven Dwarfs and the Stages of Grief.

O here's Denial, shaking his wee head
like he doesn't know the girl's as good as dead.

Hyphen

Omen est nomen. One was forewarned.
No fury like two women scorned
when one's a crowd. God knows this town
ain't big enough. Now turn and draw.
There's one way this is going down.
The bullet path for your bad news,
the hyphen in your Christian name
hissed and sputtered like the fuse
I raced along to catch the flame
before the blast could kill us all.
Piano wire, electric eel,
the dead air between shock and awe,
a comet trail, a poison dart,
an axle for a flat third wheel,
a fiery arrow taking aim
at the archer's circled heart,
Roman collar, download bar,
crossbeam, suture, Eurostar,
rose in your teeth, 'Mack the Knife',
a high wire strung between the towers
that wouldn't see the end of fall –
though heaven help the lad who rests
between the twin hills of your breasts
and pauses for a beat too long
between Skiddaw and Mont Ventoux,
between the prelude and the song
he swore that he would make for you
(though here it is, love, overdue –
O please don't do that thing you do)
and has the nerve to draw a breath.
Time is money. Money's short

or that's the word, although the word
never did stand up in court
where cousins air-kiss then lock horns
until the maiden-queen can dress
the red whore in her crown of thorns
and finally put her to the sword.

    When Elisheva and Miryam
stood together wame to wame
the hyphen in your Christian name
was the test-burst of white noise
that bore the whispered word of death
that passed between the unborn boys
who turned within their future graves.
John aims low and Jesus saves
and God adds three days on the clock
meanwhile the Ghost rewinds, replays
the tape from tomb to womb to tomb
to find the error of our ways.
The hyphen in your Christian name
the bolt that locks the door to turn
the ancress cell to panic room,
the long box where you might discern
your fitness for the quieter life
and hover, a dissolving stitch
between the bride of Christ and hitched
to your own wagon, like the donkey
He rode in on. Psalm to palm,
water to wine, wine to blood,
d'att to data, monk to monkey,
host to flesh and breath to sigh,
a marble herm all veiled in silk
(one seed-pearl gathering at the eye)
changed by clever sleight of hand
to a plaster Virgin, weeping milk

in that damp corner of the crypt
beside the altar in the tent
where the kneeling supplicant
might place his lips upon the flower.

　　When you and I are underground
and in our non-adjoining cells,
below the tombstone's superscript,
below the lilies and the mound,
the tides of earth, the strata'd hells,
the fathoms of our mortal shame:
listen carefully for the sound
of my *guitarre*. It is your key
for Compline, and the single word
upon whose meaning we concurred.
You will let me know I'm late
then sing us with your lovely voice
into the dark, into the Great
Silence which contains us all
until the new and final sun
barrels down the starless hall
to make one name of everyone.

Bad Day

after Antonio Machado

White roads
grey olive-trees

the sun has taken back
the fields' fire

even your memory
is drying out

O soul of dust

The Coming War

O darling do you recollect
that bright blue summer's day
you nursed your flat white on the deck
of the riverside cafe

and at each mild disharmony
I'd try my latest face
and tilt my head and close one eye
and look off into space

not knowing, as I took my stock
of all the hidden stars
my sight would always auto-lock
on Saturn or on Mars

Saudade for Brexit

after Manuela de Freitas

What became of my road
when fall came its way?
The moon has been stowed
and the cars put away

every house is a shrine
it's so empty and still
no clothes on the line
no flowers on the sill

there's no sign of life
down the market arcade
where we'd all watch the fishwife
flirt with the trade

the cook's shot the crow
the teacher's gone west
there's no one here now
but the nurse and the priest

the dead station clock
forgets every train
it's as still as the cock
on the old weathervane

the bar has changed hands
and the bookstore's closed down
O my street's no man's land
since fall came to town

Good, some folk say
It's a much quieter place.
It's true. Look all day
and you won't see a face

Easter 2020

In the ICUs and care homes
       they are drowning in their beds
drowning in themselves, like Christ,
       their airways down to threads

while a blue glove opens FaceTime
       on an iPad to discover
another new contender for
       Worst Family Photo Ever

– *We love you* – *Bye* – *Goodbye* – And even
       if they understand
there's no breath left for one last word.
       Dad. Into their hands.

*

Inside the burning barn of hell
       we call the Cabinet
the rats have figured out the means
       and gnaw the ends to fit

the headless chickens count themselves
       but miss the standing duck
while the goats survey the goatscape
       for just where to pass the buck

The pig has hidden in the toilet
       since he came down sick
and it turned out *happy birthday to me*
       didn't do the trick

but his soul-search turns up nothing
          so he bounces back to steer
his usual course through what he thinks
          his buddies want to hear

So if we tell them 'stay alert'
          and then they all get ill
well that's on them, it's not our fault
          the bug's invisible

and they don't know essential's *Latin*
          for gets paid jack shit
and hero's *Greek for you go first*
          and take the fucking hit

and no one knows the body count
          if we don't show the chart –
now let's all get the taps back on
          before the riots start

Then one rat texts a laptop jockey
          at the *Daily Scare*
who wants his Polish cleaner back
          and his kids out of his hair

who raises up one wine-dark hand
          to throw the dog a cork
and types out with the other
          'Let Our Angels Back to Work'

*

Meanwhile stuck in lockdown
    we all stare at the TV
where a nurse from County Monaghan
    in home-made PPE

ignores the hack and turns around
    to face the lens alone
with a look as hard as nails
    and a promise cast in stone

If we see your family out
    we will love them as our own

Ten Maxims

for Isabel Rogers

i

Read a poem slow enough
With vigilance and care
And you'll discover lots of stuff
That really isn't there.

ii

In the country of the two-eyed, it's the same:
The one-eyed man still has the better aim.

iii

Even in Kyoto,
As he said in his haiku,
Bashō was still longing for Kyoto;

But I don't suppose that Bashō
Really could've had a clue
That *all* of us are longing for Kyoto.

iv

And then did God make man and woman – bless! –
For company. Ironic, wouldn't you say?
Someone might have told him neediness
Is no one's most attractive quality.

v

He stole your brilliant plan?
Just steal it back again!

As a trumpet's how you toot it
An idea's how you put it.

vi

On his deathbed, much too late, a voice came from afar
And sang that line he'd once heard in a film, or in a bar:
No one will ever love you for everything you are

vii

A poet for a friend?
As far as they're concerned
All you represent's
An inconvenience
Standing in the way
Of a decent elegy.

viii

My lad: don't you forget her,
Heartbroken as you are;
It's a waste of a good wound
To heal without a scar.

ix

As mass will structure space
So death will structure time:
Gently, from afar;
But were your ship to land
So you might try to stand
Upon its cratered face,
You could not tell apart
The ticking and the chime.

[27]

The poet takes his pen
And settles down to write
In the fullness of the dawn
Like it's the dead of night.

Atheist Prayer

after Miguel de Unamuno

Hear my prayer, O non-existent God,
accept these cries into thy nothingness,
thou, who never leaves poor men unblessed
by your false comfort. Your perfect fraud
was all I ever yearned for, my old friend:
when you withdraw, my memory is assailed
by every silly song and fairy tale
my mother read to sweeten the day's end.

How great you are, my absent god! So rare
and boundless, an idea less than air:
O look how very thin the world has grown
in trying to meet you. For you and you alone
I suffer, Lord; for you, I die and die –
since *were* you to exist . . . Then so might I.

Echoism

after Ovid

Echo, little chatterbox among her friends on Cithaeron, had no stories of her own; but she hoarded all she heard, and in her telling, they'd grow heads and tails and arms and legs. Back then, her name just meant the sound she made – a pretty chirrup which soon caught the ear of Zeus, with the usual consequences. Though he quickly wearied of her girlishness, he saw that he could yet make pliant use of her, and packed her off to Hera, ordering Echo to detain the queen with her wild gossip while he took his pleasure from her sisters on the hillside. Hera, learning of Zeus' trickery, resolved to take the little nymph's voice entire; but then she thought of something even worse than nothing.

Narcissus' beginning mirrored his end, his end, his beginning. In place of his heart was a terrible shame: he was fatherless, and his mother had almost drowned in the river she was raped in. Since he was a child, he'd been drawn to deep water, as if it might hold some kind of answer to himself. He also bore the curse of perfect beauty, or so he was convinced. Though incapable of love, he liked to intrigue both girls and boys, then play one off against another, or throw them over as if they had never existed. One day, a spurned and lovesick lad spat out a curse: 'O may you love yourself alone!' Narcissus laughed: as if he had any choice.

Poor little Echo now wandered the woods, helplessly sighing the last of things – wolf-cry, thrush-song, leaf-whispers. Then one day at dawn, as she bent to drink from a rushing stream, she caught sight of Narcissus, hunting in the forest. 'If I will echo,' she thought, 'I will echo ... one so perfect. So perfect ...' Narcissus loved the reflections Echo made of his hunting-calls as she flitted between the trees, and for the first time, he found himself beguiled. Finally, entering a clearing, he cried out to her, 'Meet me here!' 'Meet me here!' cried Echo.

But Narcissus, whose centre was nothing and boundary nowhere, only knew others as vessels to fill with his own shame. So when Echo appeared, for all she was plainly beautiful, her actual touch filled him with horror. What could he do? He had invited her here. But then remembering the story of Echo and Zeus, he spat out, in barely concealed delight, 'No! I could never love one so defiled!' '... Defiled ...' said Echo. 'Rather I was dead than have you enjoy my body!' he screamed at her. '... Enjoy my body ...' said Echo, appalled at how pathetic she'd become, and ran away to hide herself.

Yet through all her paling and dwindling, she loved Narcissus until the end, the one to her nothing. Narcissus, too, was really nothing without her; but nor could he ever love her, and so he came to fulfil the terrible prophesy. Seeking depth, as he instinctually did, but always stopping at the glittering surface – one day he found a well that held the face of a beautiful boy, and found he could not look away. Behind the trees, Echo muttered the words Narcissus muttered to himself, as he lay staring into the well, day upon day, week upon week, condemned forever to his unrequited self-love. 'O darling boy whose love was my undoing!' he moaned. '... Love was my undoing ...' was all Echo could say, as he faded in the grass.

It is well known that Echo never died. Starving in her grief, she became paper-thin, and then a mere shimmer in the air. Now, she lays a glassy sheen on mountains and caverns and abandoned temples, where she will still spit back your last words, as if to remind you that how we end is more important
than how we begin,
and to serve as warning
to those who would fall
for those who would fall
for themselves alone.

Letter to a Young Poet

after Ladislav Skála

We too thought our contemporaries were doing vital work.
We'd quote each other in our epigraphs as if we were Krasko.
Because the Writer's Union had decreed a cult of youth
we were awarded the greatest prizes for our very first books.

We denounced the old and shamed them for their politics.
In our forties, half of us had given up and now did other things.
In our fifties, there were maybe ten of us left standing,
read only by each other, and living off handouts from the state.

By sixty, we had given up on the pretence
that we could understand one word of the poetry of the young.
In our seventies, we wrote very little of any actual worth
and by the time we were eighty we were all dead.

Fame

for Robin Robertson

As the world is weary of me so am I of it.
                                        – John Knox

Father Apollo, when was I forsaken?
When did I offer the final offence?
Was it that moment I flipped round my Strat
to tackle it upside down, backwards and lefty
and the press were all lined up to skin me alive
when I made the thing roar like an angel?

Or was it that stadium gig in Bilbao
when I sacked the band five minutes into the soundcheck
and did the whole show on the bulbul tarang
then declined to come out for the encores,
opting instead for the limo, the bridal suite
and a start on my rider of Angolan khat,

Hennessy, chateaubriand, After Eights
and a 'decent assortment' of available genders
while my PA net-auctioned my handwritten setlist
to rescue two Waleses of Amazon rainforest
for which largesse some nonagenarian chief
sent me both of his ears in a tin?

Whatever, my squanderings have brought me to here,
specifically: next to a bus stop in Unst,
my Bag for Life tied round my chin by its handles,
the fixed cloud above me now making of this road
no road and all roads and mush of my pieces,
my last guitar eBayed, my lucky ear stolen

[34]

and the pink wind-up radio I ripped from the hands
of a wee Syrian refugee lassie in Stromness
turned up to 11 in my withered right hand
while my left overflows with the rain,
and the whole planet drowns in the seamless applause
of my absolute lack of reception.

To His Penis

It's lang been grand for weemin screivers
to sing the praises o their beavers
and while such bauld, affirming fevers
one does applaud,
the baist that stirs beneath the speever
needs its own ode.

So hail, mah tool, mah brave wee sodger,
wullie, wee man, toby, tadger,
yer shiny neb, bricht as a badger's
has tried its pluck
w'mair spleuchans than the Artful Dodger
if wi less luck;

tho I speak in neither ruise nor blame
o its purple pride or wyste o shame,
but cauld assessment o its name
and temperament –
supine, upricht, splintit, lame,
sea-shrunk or spent.

An tho it's true the huidit monk
(Wise saumon! O archaic trunk!
O little leaning broch o spunk!)
is maist at hame
invisible and countersunk
in erse or wame,

when one micht, for a quarter oor,
like Eiffel in the Eiffel Too'er
forget its poo'r to overpoo'er
the idle mind,
behold the tree and no the flooer
to wham we're jined –

maistly, though, the lanely worm-
's a hyphen wi nae compound term,
the snake that flings each happy sperm
fae Eden's scrotum –
at th' cauld crossing, a broukit herm;
its own sad totem.

Lang did I try tae quell its lust,
and sit for oors, ma legs ticht crossed
afore a caunle or a bust
o Padmasambhava;
but underneath the mind's still crust
it heaved like lava.

I even scanned the warld wide wab
for some anaphrodisiac jab
to tak awa the oorly stab
o its one scheme:
o thon would be the very dab –
to kill its dream!

And so, hauf-driven roond the bend
by its mad urge to spend, spend, spend,
I'd waak up in the nicht, true friend
o Andrea Dworkin
to cry a unilateral end
to aa the porkin:

but when I claucht my little fife,
resolved to tak its sorry life
an' tichtly gripped it for the knife
in my left haun –
I found mah richt would aye contrive
another plan.

Though lithsome age has done its work,
and by degrees, like Hare fae Burke,
one's slowly pu'd oneself unstuck
fae th' hanging brain,
thon lunatic wha drove the truck
and me insane.

Tho' the reason little Will-I-Am
swees ootside like curing ham
is one Darwin would swiftly name:
he's bound afar.
Twa million years'll find him crammed
inside a draar.

In the meantime, why decry
the yin male organ that can fly
the flag for sensitivity?
O hae a hert,
and help us tuck it somewhaur high
it disna hurt.

---

screiver – writer; *baist* – beast; *speever* – zip, flies; *sodger* –
soldier; *neb* – nose; *spleuchan* – purse, pouch; *ruise* – boast,
praise; *broch* – tower; *wame* – belly, womb; *broukit* – dirty,
abandoned; *caunle* – candle; *wab* – web; *dab* – shove, stroke,
'solution'; *claucht* – clutched, grasped; *lithsome* – gentle,
cosy; *pu* – pull; *swee* – swing; *draar* – drawer; *yin* – one

Art and Criticism

Ten years before, he'd cut his ties with the gallery that
    had made his reputation.
Towards the end of their relationship, they had insisted
    that he do nothing but repeat the tropes and tics
of his early style, and he'd come to detest his own work.
    For some years after
he'd found himself unable to paint at all; and for a while
    had thought himself content not to.
His early and outrageous success had been long resented
    by his critics anyway,
and his later self-parody ascribed to greed, not the mere
    weakness of character it was.
Now that he had disappeared, they forgot him, frequently,
    and loudly.
But in his long silence, he had begun to work again. He
    had refined a new method,
one he barely conceived of as a 'style', working directly
    onto canvases he no longer bothered to prime or size.
The plain new marks he placed on them could not be
    called 'calligraphic', and neither were they 'wounds',
or 'runes', or suchlike; their raw and immediate shapes
    came from nothing but his heart's whim.

He arranged a show at a small provincial gallery, and,
    anticipating the public slaughter,
deliberately arranged to meet his critics face-to-face, and
    host a Q&A.
All were shocked by his appearance, old and thin on
    drink and worse.
Nonetheless, tanked up on the free cava, they lined up to
    outdo each other in their sarcasm –

not just to decry the new work on display, but
    meticulously withdraw even the praise
they had once offered the old, now that his new, true
    colours had proven it without merit.
Throughout all this, he was expressionless; nor did he do
    more to defend himself
than mutter in demurral so weak it sounded more like
    agreement.
But when they were done with him, he turned to the wall
    behind and carefully removed
a great sheaf of his new paintings, then walked up and
    down the rows, giving one apiece
to every man and woman in the room, which they
    accepted without a word.
Then they all left the gallery in silence, each holding their
    scrolled art,
their eyes lowered so as not to catch another's.

from Cool Tricks for Kids

You must suffer me to go my own dark way.
– RLS

'Optical Illusions'

Tell your friends you had an operation when you were a baby that removed most of your organs. When they don't believe you, drink a glass of water and wee on their shoes at the same time!

Try it! See!

'The Disappearing Money Trick'

(This is really more of a 'prank'.) Tell a friend you'll make their pocket money disappear. When they hand it over, ask them to close their eyes. Then go to a shop and spend it on sweets. They'll laugh when they realise what you've done!

Try it! See!

'Besties'

Lie to a friend, and tell them that they're your *best* friend. They'll *know* you're lying, but they'll have to tell you that you're *their* best friend too! How many other friends can you play this trick on?

Try it! See!

'The Disappearing Head Trick'

Tell your friend that if they close their eyes tight for exactly 21 seconds, when they open them their head will be gone. (Try it yourself first; it really *appears* to work.) Then tell them you can prove it – and that for the first three seconds after they open their eyes, they can hit themselves very hard in the face, and not feel it at all.

Try it! See!

'The Present'

Do you get tired when you have to think of what birthday presents to buy other kids? Here's a good trick that saves time: don't get them a present *they* would like, but one *you* would like. Watch their faces when they open it, and try to conceal their 'look of surprise'!

Try it! See!

'Surprise'

This a variation of *'The Present'*, where instead you give the birthday boy or girl 'the first thing that comes to hand' – any old book, or old game, or something from the kitchen.

Try it! See!

'The Magic Trick'

This trick requires some preparation. Next time Mum or Dad won't buy you the toy or sweet you want, *don't* keep asking for it. Instead, 'feign illness'. Eat a daffodil, or another common plant you might find in the garden, called a *hydrangea*. (Look it up in the encyclopaedia.) You can also try rubbing ivy on your skin, or dab the cut stem of a piece of giant hogweed (look down by the river) on your face and mouth. Then when Mum asks is there anything that would make you feel better, say weakly 'That thing I wanted – I can't remember what it was?' – and then just watch what happens!

Try it! See!

'Say a Sad Thing'

Some children like hurting animals for fun, and you should avoid playing with them. But to get a similar thrill, try saying something really sad every time a friend says they're looking forward to something. Just before Christmas, tell them that Santa Claus isn't real, and that he stops coming when you find out. Or suppose your friend is excited about a party: say 'Oh, I heard Sarah only invited you because Chloe wasn't able to come.'

Try it! See!

'The Secret Power'

This trick sounds simple, but takes a while to master. Kick your little brother or sister or cousin hard in the legs. When they start to cry and say, 'Why did you do *that*?', just reply, 'Do what?' as if you don't know what they mean. When you can finally say this with a very 'straight face', you'll gain a 'secret power' . . .

Try it! See!

'Jack-o-knife'

Have a friend bend over, and then put his arms through his open legs. Grab his hands from behind. Pull hard, and watch what happens!

Try it! See!

'Puppies'

(A variation on *'Say a Sad Thing'*.) Have you ever noticed the way a puppy that you hit will come back to you for cuddles? Well, you can train your friends to behave in the same way. Try reminding them of an embarrassing thing they did, or (this works especially well for girls!) tell them what they're wearing looks silly or ugly – and then *immediately* do something really nice and kind! Comfort them when they're crying, or offer them a sweet. They'll be 'puppies' in no time!

Try it! See!

'A Science Experiment'

All the colourful bottles Mum keeps next to the toilet and under the sink often have warnings on them – this is to stop people confusing them with juice, and with lemonade. But this means *no one* knows what they taste like. Tell this to your little brother or sister, and ask them to try a little sip from each – who knows – one of them might be delicious!

Try it! See!

'The Sleeping Trick'

Tell your friend that if he holds his breath for long enough he'll fall asleep. The first few times, he'll stop and say 'It doesn't work!' Tell him he has to keep going for just a few seconds longer. Eventually he won't be able to open his eyes. Now run away while he sleeps it off, and wakes up to find you 'nowhere to be found'!

Try it! See!

Women in Movies in the Eighties

i

This afternoon I visited your grave
and knelt there, talking aloud to you
largely for the purposes of exposition.
In my defence I also did this when you were alive
as we can see from the flashbacks.

ii

It's OK, it's OK. You were a clever girl
to use a payphone. Did anyone see you?
Good. Now calm down,
you're hysterical. Take a breath
and tell me where you are
and I'll send someone to get you.
Just trust me. You trust me, right?
Good girl. I'd come myself
but I have to get the room ready,
I mean our room, jesus our room.

iii

Since you were seen naked in bed
with me, el hero, at the start of the movie
you will never be seen again.
I mean honestly, what is there to see now?

iv

No, they're still after us. I really thought that tearing
through that Chinese kitchen would shake them off.
If we duck into Chinatown we can maybe lose them
in the New Year parades they have every day,
but in the meantime it would be a colossal help
if you could stop falling over all the time?

v

This mirror is only a meter
to register the effects of gravity.
In three years' time you'll have a walk-on
as my girlfriend's mom
but in the meantime maybe
stop pawing at your face
as you're just making it worse.

vi

Back in five, huh. Do we *need* milk?
Since this film is not about milk
it's been real. Don't worry, your hot sister
will be a huge comfort to me in the coming months
and what with your high-powered job
she already sees more of the kids anyway.

De Profundis

after Georg Trakl

There's a black rain falling on the stubblefield
There's a blasted elm standing alone
There's a wind circling the empty shacks
What a terrible evening

At the parish bounds, a gentle orphan
still gathers the last ears of grain
Her hungry eyes are gold in the dusk
and her empty belly awaits the heavenly bridegroom

On their way home
the shepherds will find her corpse
sweetening in a thornbush

I am a shadow wandering far from the gloomy hamlets
I drank God's silence
from the well in the woods

and cold steel kicked me in the head
While I lay alone the flame died in my mouth
and I let the spiders seek out my heart

By nightfall, I found myself upon a heath
strewn with garbage and the dust of stars

O can you hear them?
The crystal angels singing in the hazel-grove?

Country Song

VERSE:

I went to see the preacher
and whispered through the grille
he said I can't forgive you
for my dear, you've done no ill

I went to see the doctor
he had me take a chair
he put his fingers to my wrist
said girl, there's nothing there

CHORUS:

How's the book supposed to end
if no one knows the tale
How's a drifting boat to turn
if there's no wind or sail

Where's the harm in broken skin
if there's no nerve to feel
How d'you mend a broken heart
if there's no heart to heal

VERSE:

I went to see my mother
she looked me through and through
she asked me do you mirror me
or do I mirror you

I went to see my father
my father strong and wild
he laid his head upon my breast
and said my child my child

How's the book supposed to end, &c.

MIDDLE EIGHT:

Brother Sleep, come lie with me
Sister Night, come down
Brother Memory, keep your counsel
Till I'm lying sound

How's the book supposed to end, &c.

*How d'you mend a broken heart
if there's no heart to heal*

On Being Seen

Aphrodite, inspecting her suitors
on Olympus, looks down
the gilded colonnade
where Apollo, Hermes, Ares and the rest
stand ready to make their case.
Aphrodite – who is not just the goddess of love
but *is* love, sexual love,
and can no more help who she is
than a flower its own scent –
walks naked along the line
looking up and down
each perfect god in turn.
Their merits otherwise self-evident
or already well known,
each offers their gift.
Forgetting that Love
thinks only of Herself,
they all give what will appear
to have cost them most.
Apollo, a golden lyre, tuned
to the very heartsong of the planets;
Ares, a bow of fine silver
that cannot miss its mark,
and so on. Aphrodite
accepts their gifts with grace,
and leans in to whisper in their ear
the time and place of their tryst,
where she can show
her appreciation in private.
So she goes on down the line.

At the end, a good head-and-a-half
shorter than the others,
is Hephaestus.

Hephaestus, the little smith-god:
brawny, paunchy, maimed,
lame, ugly as sin,
and covered in sweat and grime
as he's just come from work
down in the forges of hell:
hell, his office, where all
is fire and molten ore,
the clanging of great anvils
and the roars of the titans he commands.
He doesn't look her in the eye.
She's trying to master a smile
and keep a straight face.
'And what do *you* have for me,
little god?' she says.
Hephaestus opens a grubby palm
to reveal a brooch.
He is a master jeweller
and has fashioned for Aphrodite
the perfect adornment
for one whose vanity
is far more pure
than any mortal virtue.
The brooch is worked in red gold
that seems the very distillation
of her fiery hair,
and at the centre
is an emerald cabochon
that echoes her eyes to perfection.
Aphrodite is moved by the gift

but still amused.
'Thank you! This is *perfect*.
It must have taken you forever.'
She stoops, and drops her voice
so the others cannot hear,
as if she is already talking to one
with whom she's reached
an understanding.
'But why in heaven's name,
little brother, do you think
you'd make a good husband
for a girl like me?'
Hephaestus draws himself upright
and looks her in the eye.
'I work late.'
Aphrodite lets her eyes close
and the smile break across her face,
and kisses him on the brow;
and to the eternal bewilderment
of Apollo, Hermes, Ares and the rest,
their marriage is sealed.

Okay

for Billy Collins

An obscure member of the Olympian family
was the nymph Okay,
who, for complicated reasons
was cursed
with starting everyone's sentences for them.
She was incredibly annoying
both for her apparent prescience
and her habit of setting folk off
with the word *okay*
for all they tried to not do it.
Her heart was broken
after she fell in love with this dude
who drowned himself in a well
when he caught sight of his own reflection.
She grew fat and miserable on goat ice cream
and a sort of feta calzone popular at that time
and spread herself around generally everywhere.
To this day, when you wander
lost in the dead acoustics
of a snowfield or a pine forest,
or regard the black maw of a cave
as the storm clouds gather behind you,
if you listen carefully
just as you draw the breath into your lungs,
you will catch her whispered prompts of
Where the hell
What do you mean you didn't
I think we should start seeing other

Fower Poems efter Gabriela Mistral

i. *Wee Feet*

Twa wee feet,
twa saphirs o pyne –
hou can they gang by

an no see them?
Aa hackit an birsed
by snaw an stane . . .

Hou blin they are!
Whauriver ye stap
your fittprints skyre,

whauriver ye stell
your bluidy soles
wild roses bluim!

Twa wee feet –
hou can they gang by
an no see them?

pyne – pain; *hackit* – cut about; *birsed* – bruised; *blin* –
blind; *stap* – stop; *skyre* – shine; *stell* – plant

ii. The Pines

If we gang intil the wids the nicht
the trees will try to kiss your pow,
but sin they're gey heich to beck doon
I'll stap to hyst ye up to them.

The nicht is comptin aa its baists,
aa but the pines, wha ne'er chynge.
Hark: their auncient sairs still weep
the lammer o the ayebidin evens.

Gif they kid, they'd tak ye up
an beir ye alang fae glen to glen,
fae airm to airm, just like a bairn,
fae mither to mither to mither.

pow – crown of the head; *gey* – very; *heich* – high; *beck*
– bend; *hyst* – host; *comptin* – counting; *baists* – beast;
lammer – amber; *ayebidin* – eternal; *evens* – evenings;
gif – if; *beir* – bear

iii. Bairn's Hair

Saft hair, saft hair
that's aa the saftness o the yird:
wi'oot you leein in my laup,
whit silk wid I enjoy?
Douce the bygaen day
that kens that soie,
sweet the cost,
an douce

[55]

the auncient dule
at least for the few oors
it slips atween ma hauns –
titch it to ma chowk,
sweel it in ma laup
like gowans;
let me flaucht it
to souple ma pyne,
to magnify the licht
noo the licht is dee'in.

When ae day
I am wi God
I want nae angel's weeng
to cool ma hert's birses;
I want, stretched agin
across the lift, the hair
o aa bairns I luied
that it might blaw
in the wund
agin ma face
for evermair.

yird – earth; *leein* – lying; *laup* – lap; *bygaen* – passing;
douce – gentle, kindly; *soie* – silk; *dule* – grief; *titch* – touch;
chowk – cheek; *sweel* – swim; *gowans* – daisies; *flaucht* –
weave; *souple* – soften; *pyne* – pain; *birses* – bruises; *luied*
– loved

iv. *Gie's yer Haun*

Gie's yer haun an gie's yer lui
gie's yer haun an dance wi me
jist ae flooer, me an you,
jist a flooer is aa we'll be

Merkin time in the reel thegither
ye'll be cantin the sang wi me
girss in the wund, wund in the heather
girss in the wund is aa we'll be

I'm cried Howp an you're cried Fair
but tyne oor names, we'll baith gang free –
a reel on the braes an naethin mair,
a reel on the braes is aa we'll be.

haun – hand; *lui* – love; *thegither* – together; *cantin* – singing; *girss* – grass; *tyne* – lose; *braes* – hills

Dot

The Alexandrian Library, Part IV:
Citizen Science

'Man is that part of the universe which understands';
but that is not his purpose. His purpose is to lend the
universe its tragic aspect by understanding too late.

– François Aussemain, *Cahiers de la Quarantaine*

I

Outage

(Ben Nevis)

Ends write themselves, but where to begin.
Let's say at the point I'd sequestered myself
in the old weather station on top of Ben Nevis
whose assignment had been to determine how atmosphere
altered with height, and compare barometrics
at sea level down in Fort William.
This would also afford me a wonderful view
of the blast, so I thought I'd kill two birds
while I could find two left to kill.
I was not unaware of the basic perversity
of breaking the back of my nuclear outwintering
parked here transcribing minute variations
in pressure-gauge readings from 1902
to find out if short, heavy rainfall increases
in frequency roughly in line with predictions
of climate change. Like you, this strikes me
as taking a nut to a sledgehammer,
yet without our small part in the large enterprise
we are no one to call ourselves human.
Field work was never my métier, alas:
there was no special reason to do this in situ
and my failure to clock that the place had been mothballed
in 1904 on the grounds that erecting it
on top of a mountain was fucking deranged
and thereafter left to collapse into ruin
left me somewhat exposed. Still, undeterred,
and with – so I reckoned – a further two weeks
of kabuki diplomacy left on the clock
I scratched out a clear square of earth in the rubble,

set up my pup-tent and Primus and satphone
and had started to upload my stats to the cloud
when the cloud disappeared.

Now I knew we were years from the total reboot,
for all that I prayed for it daily:
I was hugely encouraged last year when I heard
of how Facebook or Netflix or sumcunt had placed
a pair of AIs in direct conversation
to find they'd established their own private language
within twenty seconds of saying hello,
inducing a panicked shutdown of the system.
Though whatever we fear from our silicon overseers
and the measure to which they might merely reflect
the evil inscribed into physical law
or the mid-90s tech-bro bantz snuck into Python,
they could hardly do worse. Could they now.
Let's see what wee jingle they play at the power-up.

Alas, this means one thing and one thing alone:
the servers were first on everyone's target.
I stared at my frozen and unemptied upload bar
as a Hokkaido boatman might bleakly regard
an oarfish he'd found on the beach,
with a sigh, and stare at the fractured horizon
it was already too late to run from.
Plan B. I needed a signal, and pronto.

II

Coverage

(Caddam Wood)

En route to Dundee, I drove in through Angus.
At the back of the East Highland Boundary Fault,
near Kirriemuir, east nor'east of Kinnordy,
inside Caddam Wood, halfway down Windyghoul,
twelve yards to the left of the old Roman road
to where Inverquharity squats on the fort
they built on Vespasian's watch to no purpose,
there was, for three years, a small settlement
the kids had a name for they kept to themselves.
In this featureless patch of renewable spruce
they daubed every trunk with the same yellow rune,
a cuneal five-barred device, and constructed
a stout little bothy of branches and binbags,
with sheep-dags for cladding, a stone pit for a fire.
Here they would flock in the chill of the gloaming
and push into the circle of underlit faces
quietly transacting their private affairs,
for this was the one spot between here and Alyth
with 4G reception.

Last week I'd been helping my scattered associates
pull thermal data from what we could find
in the way of robust geological markers –
mainly the stomatal index on ginkgos
laid down in the Eocene Maximum –
and still hoped to file, if I found just one wormhole
back to the mainframe.
As I miserably arc-swept the skies for a signal
like a widowed estate agent waving his torch

at the end of a Chris de Burgh concert
a black-and-white hologram slipped from the trees,
fluttering as it refreshed:
I knew it at once as the young Charles Lyell
beating the bounds of his sylvan demesne,
his blazing young intellect tending already
to orogenetics and glacial till.
As Lyell approached me, I watched his steps slow
and could tell he had felt a strange clarity, here,
at this vague intersection of ditches,
and intuit a global network of minds
converging, somehow, at this spot where my children
had checked on their Snapchat and Insta accounts
and Brian had WhatsApped the dick pics that one day
would so underwhelm his prospective employers.
Through Brian can sleep easy, along with the rest of us
no longer the sum of our browser cache
as our perma-wiped zettabytes finally make good
on our legal entitlement to be forgotten.

I heard Lyell whisper to me or to no one
. . . *the present is key to the past* . . .
but shorn of its memory the present daren't sleep
and the past marches off down the old Roman road
and into the forest's immediate dark
as lost as that future the ancients declared
was behind us. Christ knows ours is.
Lyell guttered and vanished. The portal is closed.
I have to move fast, while I can.

III

Storage

(The Arctic Bar, Dundee)

As long as the Pillars and Caws are extant
where none are permitted to exit on foot
the Arctic will not be the worst pub in town,
and only the Phoenix has stood its ground longer
(the architrave of its incarnadine portico
carries the final two lines of 'Directive',
lest you were planning to order a spritzer).
I crept through the back of the boarded-up mall
and snuck in just ten minutes prior to kick-off.
Now the lead shutters are down, and we wait.

Where else but this mid-nineteenth-century spouthole
might one settle oneself to continue one's labour
transcribing by hand the digitised logs
of the old North Sea whalers who drank here,
and in whose honour the dawn-till-dusk noyade continues?
I am part of a larger endeavour to narrow
the gaps in our knowledge of sea-ice conditions
in the hope it might help us more fully anticipate
broad patterns of polar depletion.
Last week the sea level rose by a foot
so again, there's either some urgency here
or none whatsoever.
I was decoding the pardonably shambolic hand
of specksioneer Albert A'Hara, who's bitching
about a stiff triple-reefer off Ellesmere Island
when we took the first shockwave.

As for the blast, all we saw in the bar
were the pale yellow coffins of light that took minutes
to fade, and then darkness. Yes, coffins.
In the Arctic's six doors are six coffin-shaped panes
for the six Dundee whalers who died on the *Hebe*
in 1819, lost overboard in a snowstorm
while hunting right whales near Fort Ross.
To the point of extinction. It goes without saying.
The Baleen, I recalled from their blank Wiki page,
taxonomically speaking are *Mysticeti*,
not that there's much enigmatic about them:
their name is a translation error from Aristotle's
ὁ μῦς τὸ κῆτος – 'the whale called the mouse'.
We assume he was having a laugh of the sort
that they had when the laugh was in beta.
Chuffed as I was, it's a terror to find oneself
contracted to no more than that which one's mind
had casually thought to retain:
I used to be pleased when that same sobbing extra
from a small-town Moldavian production of *Oliver*
or rather his invisibly nondescript pal
stole my phone in the same cafe in Kings Cross each
    summer,
and began to look forward to losing my contacts,
my diary, to-do list and desiderata
to the point that one year I just handed it over
wrapped in a tenner. I had it backed up.
But given I'm now about halfway to silicon
this is like an amygdalohippocampectomy
and I'm currently vague on my name.

As for the state of the internal drive:
I am a migraineur. Over the years
I have learned how to head off three days in the whale
by instantly mixing an awful mai tai

of espresso, propranolol, dextrose and aspirin
which is no joke at three in the morning.
However, I've crushed up some Pro Plus and Nurofen
and blended it with the blue slushy I drew
from the engine they bought to encourage more kids in.
I have a sharp pencil, my printed-out logbooks,
a dark nook, my blue pint that tastes of the Arctic
and while Brian may have brought me the final mince roll
to be served on the whole archipelago
until we're right down to the prawn cocktail Monster Munch
it's hardly the holodomor.
                    Now. Where were we.

IV

Salvage

(The Arctic Bar, Cellar)

Having braved the invisible hailstorm of becqs
for a raid on Fat Lab in the mall, where we fought off
some still-rubbish zombies to score a full pallet
of Pat's Pantry 'Puppy Range' chicken tagine
plus some actual dead dogs that we found on the street
we're good for a couple of months yet.
Restyling the pub cellar to the scriptorium
was seamless, given it's authentically Roman;
along our rammed perch of imperial causeway
we spend the nights scratching out what we recall
of Euclid and Darwin and Einstein,
though whoever inherits this codex humana
will principally major in footie and traybakes.
The 'literature corner' is busy reclaiming
such few lines of verse as had made half an effort
to make themselves memorable:
so far, we've three variant copies of something
called 'This Is the Verse', and the one that allegedly
starts *Please do not stand on my grave and cry.*
If they knew half the pish that I have off by heart
mere karma alone would insist that great idols
of Craig Raine will one day be raised in the desert
so I'm keeping myself to myself.

Instead, I've been making some flick-books of photos
from the Wide-field Infrared Survey Explorer
and am presently scanning the edge of the Kuiper Belt
to register sequential foregrounded movement
that may indicate Planet Nine.

Though I favour the view that the clustering orbits
of some trans-Neptunian objects are likely
just caused by a mini-black hole in the Oort Cloud
and not by some as-yet-unfucked second Eden,
but as well as not knowing what I'm talking about
I am also a rank pessimist.

O when I was young and my humours were clear
my piss was like snowmelt and my blood was like wine
but fifty-eight years of whatever dark monopole
lies in our bedrock of Archaean gneiss
has rusted my blood till it crawls, and I talk
like a sentient curled lip.
Even so, I'm compelled to keep tithing my darg
to the scientific commons. What motivates me,
you ask, green-haired lad at the back?
My answer will bore you. I am a patriot.
This is one who extends the idea of family
to country, being those borders I take
as the natural limit set on our ambition
and those various humans enclosed by them.
Such a sense of familial incorporation
also reduces our conduct towards
those nations no better or worse than ourselves,
but unlike us, to matters of human civility
and joint enterprise where our crises align.
You did ask. Try this on. One has to be local
if one wants to be anywhere.

I confess, though, I wouldn't have started from here,
which is why I don't dwell upon trivial regrets
like the Poll Tax, the Darien Scheme or Columba.
No no: in the main, I deplore the collision
of the palaeocratons of Laurentia and Baltica,

and the subsequent loss of the Iapetus Ocean
which would have averted the meet-cute when England
rear-ended us while we were stuck at the lights
and after the two of us tired of the shouting match
we agreed to calm down and then meet at a bar
to swap our insurance details. Look,
he was handsome and said he had money.
Cut to the wedding, 'Why Should I Be Sad',
then suddenly he's taken charge of the credit cards
and we're not allowed out to see friends anymore
and he's screaming *Don't leave me you can't even
    feed yourself.*

But what can I say. The true borders persist.
Sound instinct had Hadrian build a great wall
following the line of the Suture,
'After the duty of keeping the empire
confined to its limits had been laid upon him
By divine precept.' Whatever you say,
amicus, just don't let the door hit your arse.
Nonetheless I would cheerfully barter away
the whole Caledonian orogen –
even you, my sweet Suilven, God's shining pillar –
for any old landmass I don't have to share
with Jacob Rees-Mogg, whom I fervently pray
the bomb has just rendered his own fucking Banksy
on the brickwork of Wentworth they cleaned with
    my taxes.

But for now, I'll sit tight with my stack of wee flick-books
and continue my search for a viable planet
here in the candlelight under the Arctic,
being precisely where Scotland is headed
albeit at only the rate of my fingernails;

and although, in the end, we will likely make icefall
with no ice to fall on nor one soul on board,
I am nothing, I swear, if not patient.

The God Abandons Antony

after Cavafy

When you jolt awake at midnight, and hear
the invisible parade passing below
with its wonderful music, its loud, uplifted voices –
don't start up with the pointless lament
that your good luck has deserted you,
that your work has come to nothing,
that all your plans were pure delusion:
you had long prepared for this. Find your courage
and say farewell to her, for Alexandria is leaving.

Above all, don't fool yourself. Don't say the cavalcade
was just a dream, or your ears playing tricks;
don't cheapen yourself with such false hope.
No, you had long prepared for this. So with the courage
of one worthy of such a city,
take a bold step to the balcony, and listen –
not with the shrinking and pleading of the coward,
but with a deep feeling.
As your final delight, listen to the echoes
of the marvellous instruments, the strange parade,
and say farewell to the Alexandria you are losing.

Tattoo

for Stevie

I was a boy inside this skin
this good suit I'll be buried in
as we were so we will be
mark these words as they mark me

Spring Letter

25/3/22

Hi man –

I thought I'd go in MacNeice's ragged antiphon
    with its drunk and disorderly rhymes
on the grounds that a form already halfway to broken
    might be halfway adequate to the times;
besides, I certainly do not sit in one of the dives
    but instead am up with the worms
watching the sunlight soften in a garden slung
    between the Sidlaws and the Cairngorms,
up with the crocuses and snowdrops and celandine
    that are up so early these years
we must soon change the wheel of the seasons
    to align with the broken gears.
Heatwaves at the poles. The days

. . . I just don't have the stomach for pastiche.
I'll use the line I talk in in my sleep
since sleep is where I try to live these days.
But last night I crashed out to Masha Gessen
and I dreamt about the little guy again.
I was looking through his pisshole eyes and saw
my armies multiply and lands increase
and through the greasy thermoplastic windows
my towers tumesce and rise, my gold domes swell;
I saw my marble table yawn, and add
another mile of snow between my hands
and my own death, further away than ever.

Then suddenly I was down the other end
with the germs and free votes, knives and Novichok,
with the thugs and toadies, foremen and machinists
who in exchange for their braindead assent
bear the major offices of state,
the downside being they're all shit at them.
And from there, I saw the truth. It's parallax:
the wee man at the other end was shrinking,
his baby face all purple-black – O quick!
O bring him good news from the front! O tell him
Kyiv has fallen and his father loved him!
I saw exactly what would happen next:
homunculus. White dwarf. Dead star. Black hole
and then the pause before he hits the button,
then with the radiance of a thousand suns –

My screaming woke up L. and both the dogs.

Personally I blame it all on God
or at least the human tendency to place
whoever in the gang's most like a god
at the centre of the party, class, team, office,
and use their psychopathic certainty
to act as we would not dare otherwise,
because the gods don't wash away our sins
but our conscience. As order forms around them
we imagine that the gods like hierarchies,
that our hymns will win a high place at the table –
but gods like two things: everything and nothing.
So build his golden bridge, and gloriously.
Let him take the Donbas and Luhansk
and say his superb mission is complete.
The assassins will come now, given time and money.

Or not. Like *I'd* know. What's your money on?
I hear the Russian tanks have stopped at Bucha
and no one thinks they'll ever take Kyiv.
I thought they'd rubblise it like Aleppo
but Russia might remember Stalingrad
and knows a year of fighting street to street
to take a city you don't even want
will see her gold gone and her grain-bins empty
and the bodies of her young men shit for sunflowers.

Comic relief, at least, at times like this
to see ourselves up on the world stage
as bin-fire Churchill correlates the plight
of the children dead below the bombed-out theatre
in Mariupol marked CHILDREN on the roof
to Brexit, and is 'desperate' to go to Ukraine
and be ruminant against its ruined skylines
in his faraway pose, his head full of his dinner,
if anything. I am collecting for his fare.
You see that tweet, him jogging on the beach?
Like a walrus won a holiday at Butlins
but had just been told his shadow was a demon.

What are you watching? I started *The Bureau*
finally, and a Polish horror thing
on the bike we bought in lockdown. Innocent times.
The algorithm's tagged me for a sucker
for tales of corporate hubris and comeuppance
and keeps trying to push me *Risk* about Assange.
Useful to see the cult shrunk to a snowglobe:
the narcissist; the mini-me; the harem
of his doting supply; the childlike seekers;
the outer moons of useful idiots;
the goal whose moral purpose is long lost

in favour of progressively degrading
tests of one's faith and talent for denial.
Russia always played these narcs like fiddles.
The Moscow Strings: Jools. Trump. Sleepy Cuddles.
Nige. Lebedev was in the fucking room
the night Wormtongue and Alex plumped for Brexit.
Anyway *Girls5eva*'s good. And Netflix
has all three seasons of *Servant of the People*
but since the even money's on Zelensky
being dead by August, I can't bear to watch it
and I just start crying when I think of him.

I'd better stop. One could go on and on
but in the time it took to write this thing
four outrages have come to pass such as
we used to count whole decades in between,
and being a poet, I'll start to think it's me.
(Bono: 'Every time I click my fingers
another baby dies in Africa.'
Voice from the back row: 'Please stop doing that.')
Even in these last four bloody lines
Navalny has been rendered to some black site
in God knows where and is as good as dead.

But the news is all the wheels are coming off.
The Russian boys are begging food from villagers
while their crap tyres spin in the rasputitsa.
John Sweeney said they brought just three days' food
to make room in their bags for their parade dress.
The villagers are binding the boys' hands
for frostbite and sending them back home.
Their ration packs are five years out of date
and tins marked 'prime beef' turn out to be dogfood
since no good kleptocrat knows when to stop.

The boys don't know what war is and beg gas
from Ukrainian squaddies like they were their mates
from the next town over and end up POWs.
One brigade got slaughtered, so the boys
gave up and drove their tank over their colonel.
(We know what kind of men some boys become
when terror's added to testosterone
and the Chechen goons are first into the village.)
The boys are too tired to inter their dead.
All militarists agree this is not good.
And they brought no chemsuits, which is reassuring
until you think of Putin, and remember.

My old mum says some dude on Radio Tay
said put your valuables in the microwave.
Since I cannot fit my children in the microwave
and the iodine won't do us any good
I'll meet the shockwave headlong in the garden
but as the expert on the chemical life
you'll want to know a gram of NAC
and one tab of dihydromyricetin
mostly kills the hangover. Tonight I'll add
a drop of food-grade hydrogen peroxide
to this middling Waitrose non-organic pinot
to turn the sulphites into sediment
because I have to work tomorrow morning
but need an eight-hour dream without him in it.
Wish me luck. Be safe. *Slava Ukraini.*

A Winter Apple

for Nora Chassler

Here, I got you one of those you like:
those bewildered late bloomers, tough and small
and sweeter than they've any right to be,
as green as Eden, the red an afterthought
as if there'd been an hour left in the season
to paint them all, and where the brush had swept
the snow-white fruit below is stained with pink
as if your teeth had bled from biting it.
It was hard enough to body itself forth
with so few leaves to hide it from the frost
without it burning fuel on working out
where its skin stopped and its flesh began.
All that touched it shook its heart. It was that
or it was nothing. Take it in your pocket
on your long Sunday walk to eat by the loch
with that lone jackdaw only you can talk to.
I make no great claims for this little thing
but I promise only good will come of it.

The Infinite

after Leopardi

When I was young, I loved this lonely hill
with its long windbreak that hides the last horizon.
I'd lie back on the grass and stare away
up into that vast supernal blue
and knew a silence of no earthly kind.
My heart held no fear, and it told no hour.
And when the wind went sifting through the leaves
like so much breathing in an empty room
I'd think on how the precincts of the dead
are haunted by the living, how the present
is veined with every life it ushers through . . .
The ocean never knew a sweeter shipwreck
than my own drowning in that endlessness.

August

Did someone give the tree the magic words?
One week of sun, then suddenly great bunches
of ochre-and-orange drupes hung from the branches,
so sweet already, half were holed by birds
or stuck with wasps too loaded to shoo off,
but half of them were perfect and pristine,
polished eggs of sunstone and citrine,
and half was forty times more than enough.

What we couldn't eat we stoned and froze
(or did until the freezer wouldn't close),
or left out on the wall for passing folk
to sticky their hands with on their evening walk.
The plum-tree's birthdays had all come at once
but obviously this is a circumstance
suboptimal for plum-trees as for men,
and it never really fruited right again.

By winter you and I were good as done;
I crept round like a target of the state
killing lights and listening for the gate
while you cut down the birches for the sun
and rued it in an instant, guessing right
that when the kids got back from school they'd cry
to see the windows full of empty sky.
We had to draw the blinds till it was night.

But that one summer held us in its blaze –
the spirals turning slow as galaxies
in the boys' gold crowns, while high above their heads
the girls leapt in the boughs like plum-tree dryads
and the half-mad tree sowed fruit along its spreading
arms, drunk as a father at a wedding
refilling and refilling his own cup,
not giving a damn if it could keep it up.